M000084242

Released

Jasina B. Wise

ISBN: 978-0692324059

Printed in the United States of America

Published by:

Speak Life Publishing, LLC
P.O. Box 22100
Baltimore, MD 21203
www.yelvaburley.com

DEDICATION

This book is dedicated to 3 women named Eva; my mother, my sister and my daughter. This book is dedicated to 3 men named Jason; my father, my brother and my son. Each Eva and each Jason represents a different generation and a different facet of my personality. I am who I am because of Eva and Jason.

ACKNOWLEDGEMENTS

Thank you to my family and friends who have walked with me thus far; the family members that are also friends and the friends that have become like family. I dare not mention names for surely a precious one would be missed; an error of the head and not the heart. This book is the end product of your many hours spent in conversation, prayer and presence. You have invested your time, talent and treasure in me-I love you.

CONTENTS

FOREWORD

Jasina Wise is a woman of God, who is dedicated to spreading the word of the Most High God. She is a woman of integrity, mettle, and a never wavering faith that is evident in her life. Ms. Wise is a judge out of the Old Testament in the spirit of Deborah, full of wisdom, wise words, and a heart of a warrior. She is also a woman of the New Testament lifting up the praises of God and sharing the gospel in a way that all understand.

I had the pleasure of serving on our church's music ministry with Jasina. We share a passion and appreciation for the praises of Him who wrought us. It is a wonderful experience to be a part of worship that ushers the worshippers beyond the veil and into the inner court of the Everlasting One.

Jasina has shared her passion to reach those who are trapped in the bondages of this world. Through her book *Released*, Jasina shares the Word of God to soothe those in need of comfort, encourages those feeling discouraged, and shares her life challenges so others will know they are not the only ones going through trials.

In *Released*, you will learn more about Jasina and her life but more importantly you will learn more about The One who loves you above all others.
Peace and Blessings,

Hattye C. Knight, PHR
Author of *Against Company Policy*

FOREWORD

Jesus declared that He came to give us life and life more abundantly. Yet so many born again believers are living bound. Women, children of God, of various races, different cultures, and every socio-economic background are living duplicitous lives, claiming they have the victory but living in chains of fear, depression, and the like. Reverend Jasina Wise has written a book that will compel women who've become comfortable wearing garments of slavery to strip off every weight that binds them and run the race the Lord has marked out for them, fearlessly.

Released exposes the inward struggles many women face. It is confrontational yet compassionate. Released gives every sister in Christ permission to take off every mask and to live in the Lord's truth, a truth that makes one free. The declarations throughout this book aren't clichés. They aren't trite words. They are the very word of God, active and alive, powerful and effective. As women declare their release, it will be so, in Jesus' name!

Rev. Yelva Burley
Servant

PREFACE

Released is a work of wisdom that was forged in the fire of LIFE. This book is actually a living breathing document that was birthed from the womb of a real woman who responds to real situations sometimes successfully and sometimes not so admirably. Released had to be lived for fifty years before it could be birthed into the literary realm. Each chapter represents a season of life. I needed to live for half a century before I could become comfortable with the transparency required to release this to public scrutiny. I no longer define myself by what others think or say about or to me. I am confident that God loves me and that He will never leave me. I am accepted in the Beloved. I am aware that I probably have more years behind me than I do ahead of me. This is not a declaration of sorrow but a proclamation of intent. I have work that must be done and I intend to work while it is still day…for the night will come when this woman will translate from labor to reward. Hallelujah!

Released is a work of wisdom; words and illustrations that challenge you to breakdown whatever has imprisoned you. The "whatever" may be internal or external. The "whatever" may actually be a noun. Remember a noun is a person, place or thing? Whatever the warden- Released is your map to freedom. Yet Released goes even further than just showing you the way to freedom. The prisoner must first acknowledge that he is imprisoned. The most insidious captor will seek to hide the fact that the prisoner is imprisoned. Oh the subtlety of a prison fashioned with hidden bars, for if the prisoner does not believe that he is confined he will never seek freedom. If confinement has been assigned the veneer of normalcy why explore release? This book will challenge you to challenge yourself. This book is for man, woman, boy or girl. This work of wisdom is multi-generational, cross-cultural, non gender specific, and without regard to socio-economic status, location or locale.

I challenge you to read the chapters as you see fit. There is no requirement to go in order. Read and reflect, after reflection - journal and pray. This book is for you and or for you to get into the hands of someone else. This is a work of wisdom. This is a map to freedom-to live Released.

INTRODUCTION

Release is different. I know how to wear depression or loneliness or any of the other garments in the Table of Contents. I know how to function when wearing those garments. As a matter of fact I wore those garments so long that they felt like I was born to wear them. I functioned well in spite of them. I actually excelled in some areas of my life in spite of and sometimes because of them. For example, the need to please people will compel you to say "YES" to every request and sacrifice your own health, finances, and relationships to always do a good job.

The unbalanced life can actually appear very accomplished on the surface. The problem with the surface is that it will never prevent what is directly under it from eventually surfacing...

Yes, release is different. Romans 12:2 (Amp) says,
Do not be conformed to this world (this age), [fashioned after and adapted to its external, superficial customs], but be transformed (changed) by the [entire] renewal of your mind [by its new ideals and its new attitude], so that you may prove [for yourselves] what is the good and acceptable and perfect will of God, *even* the thing which is good and acceptable and perfect [in His sight for you]. I had to learn a "new normal" upon my release. The power of God released me and I had to learn how to live as a free person. The children of Israel had to learn how to live as free people. Did you ever wonder why the early books of the Old Testament are so laborious and specific? God had to teach a people how to transform their thinking from slave to free. I can

relate to some of the early murmurings of the Israelites. Consider Exodus 16-"Moses, at least we had food to eat in Egypt (let's not mention the bondage thing right now...) Yes, at least we had food to eat! These are the cries of a free person who still has a slave mentality. Did you forget the overseer's whip? Yes it may take some time before your mind catches up to your new position. The mind can play tricks on you. Hindsight can be delusional. Maybe the abuse wasn't really all that bad. Maybe? Lord, give me a new mind. Give me the mind of Christ. May I no longer think like a victim but think as a victor. I must have the thoughts of one who is above and not below.

I am RELEASED.

Through the years You and I were friends.

Seemingly the best, You were there at every stage of my life

As a young girl I remember you,

the memory is faded but I know that it was you

As a teenager I can remember your laughter,

it filled our room

In college you walked the campus right beside me

You were there at the wedding and in the days that followed

You were with me at each child's birth.

As I struggled with parenthood you were there

As I accepted middle age you were there.

My oldest most constant companion...

Good bye forever.

Fear, I reject you.

Your assignment is over.

FEAR

False Evidence Appearing Real

Fear is a lie.

It is a lie spoken to your mind and your heart. It is a lie which is believed by your heart and your mind. Your body believes fear. Your heart rate may increase; your stomach may cramp. Some sweat, develop headaches and may even weaken in the knees. False Evidence. Evidence is used to prove something, right? Fear attempts to prove that which is actually a lie, an untruth. How can you prove a lie? A lie is proven only with another lie. Only truth will disprove a lie. Fear is based on a lie, an untruth.

False (untrue) Evidence Appearing Real

Appearances can change based on surroundings. Lighting can affect appearance. Is it bright? Is it foggy? Is it midnight dark? The type of light that is directed to the evidence will determine how the evidence appears. Let me explain. The Bible speaks of having a form of godliness but denying the power thereof (2 Timothy 3:5-7).

> When you are dwelling (living) in the true light, false evidence will appear as false. You will recognize it as false evidence appearing real.

If your "godliness" is a watered down muted form, then the light shining through you is muted (dull). When you shine a dull light visibility is limited. You can miss the details. You don't actually see the whole picture. False Evidence doesn't look false; it looks real. The muted light doesn't let you see the inconsistencies that can make the false seem real.

If you are experiencing unfounded fear, check your light. Is it the true light of Jesus Christ or have you picked up a muted form of godliness? Lack of prayer, minimal reading of God's Word, and infrequent uncommitted fasting are signs that you may have a "form of godliness." In this state, the false evidence will appear real. Much prayer, frequent reading of God's Word and committed fasting as a way of life will keep you in contact with the true light of Jesus Christ. "Thy word is a lamp unto my feet and a light unto my path."
Psalm 119:105

"Then spake Jesus again unto them saying, "I am the light of the world; he that followeth me shall not walk in darkness, but shall have the light of life." John 8:12

When you are dwelling (living) in the true light, false evidence will appear as false. You will recognize it as false evidence appearing real. You will be an example of 2 Timothy 1:7:

For God hath not given us the spirit of fear, but of power and of love and of a sound mind.

Released from Fear.

NEXT STEPS

Do you recognize FEAR as a hindrance in your life? Are you often hesitant to take even the most cautious chance? Have past failures caused you to second guess yourself? Have you settled for the sure thing even though your heart is yearning for more? Have you convinced yourself that you are satisfied because you are afraid of change? If your self talk sounds like …Well it's really not that bad. I'm better than most people in my situation. I am too old to try that. I am too young to achieve that yet. Do you allow the giant named "What If" to stop you from crossing the bridge to greater? Be RELEASED from fear!

Pray and ask God to show you the areas of your life that are being hindered by fear. There may be times when it is best for you to proceed with caution. However you must differentiate those times from instances when fear has impaired your mobility. Prayer will illuminate the presence of fear, once the fear has been identified ask God to permanently remove it from you and replace it with boldness.

Be consistent and deliberate about removing fear from your life. Don't even allow small fears to persist. Seek accountability from people you can trust and or professional Godly counselors. I will not deliberately stick my hand into the mouth of a snake but I am not fearful of them. I am cautious and wise, but not fearful.

PRACTICAL APPLICATION

Identify at least one area of your life where you have been walking in fear. It may be fear of speaking up in group conversations, fear of walking near large statues, fear of spiders or fear of continuing your education. For the next 21 days write down instances where you confronted a fear. It may be as simple as going online and researching available funding sources for education. You might go to a toy store and pick up a stuffed spider and quietly declare that God has delivered you from the fear of spiders. You could begin specifically praying for God to allow you to walk by a specific large statue. You could simply audibly say "I agree" to someone else's statement the next time you are in a large group conversation. Do you get it? It is a 21 day commitment to take a baby step in confronting fear.

The journey of a thousand miles begins with a single step. (Lao-tzu, Chinese philosopher)

WWW (What Went Well)

Use this page to notate what went well as you made practical application of the next steps being RELEASED from FEAR.

Dear...

What would you say if you had to write a note of encouragement to someone who needs to be RELEASED from Fear?

Lest We Forget

Use this section to write a poem or other piece for recitation, compose a song, draw a cartoon, take a photograph and tape it here or any other type of creative expression that will trigger remembrance of the need to remain RELEASED from FEAR.

Purposeful Prayer

Incorporate what you have learned into your daily prayers. Locate relevant scriptures and write them down as you commit them to memory for inclusion in times of prayer.

Loud voices

Raised fists

Slammed doors

Thrown dishes

Hang up the phone

No one answer the door

Anger's been evicted.

You don't live here anymore.

James 1:19-20
This you know, my beloved brethren. But everyone must be quick to hear, slow to speak *and* slow to anger; for the anger of man does not achieve the righteousness of God.

Ephesians 4:26-27
Be angry, and yet do not sin; do not let the sun go down on your anger, and do not give the devil an opportunity.

Proverbs 15:1
A gentle answer turns away wrath. But a harsh word stirs up anger.

Ephesians 4:31-32
Let all bitterness and wrath and anger and clamor and slander be put away from you, along with all malice. Be kind to one another, tender-hearted, forgiving each other, just as God in Christ also has forgiven you.

ANGER

I see the seeds of anger beginning to take root in the next generation. Mean girls and mean boys. Offspring desensitized to pain by too many hours of primetime movies which show murder after murder separated by 30 second T.V. commercials selling fast food and fast cars.

The more carnage the better.

Desensitized by the evening news "the 25th murder of the year." No mention of the grieving spouse or parentless child. Desensitized by music lyrics which compartmentalize each body part, each sex. Music so loud that I only feel the beat. I observe from the outside looking in. So much stimulation. Over stimulation. I lose myself. Who can I talk to? What is this that I'm feeling? Don't touch me. Don't look at me. Why isn't anyone touching me? Why doesn't anyone see me? Internal press. External pressure.

I am about to blow...

Where does Anger come from? Why are some people predisposed to anger? Is it hereditary? The discussion could flow in several directions but the bottom line is that Anger will control you if you don't recognize it as the destructive force it is. You have to be honest with yourself and admit that this is something over which you have, in the past, been powerless. Once you *Trace* it to the source, you can *Face* it without pretention and *Erase* the negative outcomes.

> Once you *Trace* it to the source, you can *Face* it without pretention and *Erase* the negative outcomes.

You have to admit to yourself that your charged responses are reflective of your own lack of self-control. Stop. Breathe. You cannot control the other person or even the situation as a whole. You can only control You. You have the power to stop saying words that hurt. Stop slamming doors, punching walls, driving aggressively, and drinking recklessly. To commit an act out of anger is to allow the devil opportunity for victory in your life. Take back your Power. Breathe.

Anger Be Gone.

<u>NEXT STEPS</u>

Are you ready to admit that Anger has negatively affected your life? Will you admit that you tend to overreact and under apologize? Those who should respect you are actually afraid of you because you allow anger to speak for you. Anger has been your default but that can change today. The past is past, today pray and ask God to forgive you for acts of anger. Ask God to allow those you have hurt to forgive you. Ask God to help you to forgive yourself.

Remember **Trace It Face It Erase It**? Pray and ask God to reveal the root of your anger. Anger is a feeling. What initially caused you to become angry? You respond in anger to specific triggers. If I feel like I am being lied to I explode because my ex told me lies all the time. When someone does something I told them not to do I explode because I feel like they are saying I am not important enough to be listened to. Growing up I always felt like no one took me seriously because I wasn't as athletic as my older brothers. These are just a few examples of what may be the root of your anger. Prayer to God and committed times of quiet reflection will be needed to identify the root or roots.

PRACTICAL APPLICATION

Identify at least one area of your life where you have been walking in anger. Angry exchanges with your children, spouse, classmates, co-workers or siblings. For the next 21 days write down instances that triggered anger in you. Identify why you were feeling angry. Write down why you respond in anger to that trigger. Let your explanation be introspective, not because the other person did thus and so but because I felt this or that. It is a 21 day commitment to begin identifying anger and its roots. It is the process of RELEASE from Anger.

"It is wise to direct your anger towards problems -- not people; to focus your energies on answers -- not excuses."
William Arthur Ward

<u>WWW (What Went Well)</u>

Use this page to notate what went well as you made practical application of the next steps being RELEASED from ANGER.

Dear...

What would you say if you had to write a note of encouragement to someone who needs to be RELEASED from Anger?

Lest We Forget

Use this section to write a poem or other piece for recitation, compose a song, draw a cartoon, take a photograph and tape it here or any other type of creative expression that will trigger remembrance of the need to remain RELEASED from ANGER.

Purposeful Prayer

Incorporate what you have learned into your daily prayers. Locate relevant scriptures and write them down as you commit them to memory for inclusion in times of prayer.

RAGE

Anger is a feeling. I have been wronged or offended.

Rage is a verb; it denotes action. It is retaliation for that which brought me to the point of anger. I feel anger and now you will feel the consequences of my rage.

Red, boiling red overflowing.

Boiling over, spilling over

Past the point of return

Clear the path, everything

Anyone in my way –

You have been warned!

Anger has given birth to RAGE.

The Bible instructs us to be angry but sin not. The sin is rage. When angry do no sin. Do not ever let your wrath [rage](your exasperation, your fury or indignation) last until the sun goes down (Ephesians 4:26).

When we act upon or actually out of anger, that is rage. Punching walls, slapping your children or spouse in the face, slashing the tires or breaking the windows of your ex's vehicle. Taking all of the clothes out of your offender's closet, dousing the clothes with gasoline and setting them on fire, spray painting graffiti on someone's car.

Rage, rage, rage.

The unsatisfied fire that refused to be quenched. "I am the victim so I have earned the right to victimize!" These are the words of one who has not surrendered their pain to Jesus. Unsurrendered pain fertilizes the egg of anger and rage is born. Rage can take on a life of its own. It will cause you to react in ways normally uncharacteristic. Ways which will cause you to reflect in regret. "How could I have done that" or "I don't believe I did that." Rage is the progeny of unrepented or unsurrendered sin and anger.

Lest we propagate rage any further let us surrender our anger to God. It is okay to be angry in some situations. Your anger can be justified but your rage is never apropos. A healthy response to that which caused the anger is possible without rage. Rage is an irrational response. It is not sinful to be angry (this should never be a constant state for a mature person). A mature person is able to self regulate and respond to anger in a non-threatening way. Immaturity will allow anger to become rage. Ignorance will do the same!

Rage be gone!

NEXT STEPS

In most instances you can read this book in any order. It is not necessary to follow a strict order, but in this case I advise you to read the chapter on Anger if you have not already done so. Unchecked Anger becomes rage so you must deal with Anger to become effectively released from Rage. As you are released from Anger you will simultaneously be confronted with the release from Rage. You are not powerless over Rage. You have access to the Blood of Jesus Christ to assist you. I don't care how long you have been operating in Rage. It does not matter the root, there is Power In the Blood of Jesus! Call upon the Lord right now. Begin to uproot this characteristic from your life and instead plant the seeds of a peaceful character. You can do this in the Name of Jesus! Pray and Declare, RELEASE from Rage!

PRACTICAL APPLICATION

Identify times when you have acted out of rage. How does it make you feel to reflect on those times? Write down an alternate response to whatever caused the rage. For the next 21 days keep a written account of times when you acted out in rage. Do you notice any recurrences? Are there certain people, places or things always around when you act out in rage? What were you doing right before the rage? Where were you? Who were you with? What was your physical state? Were you trying to function with a lack of sleep? What was your financial state? Rage was in your past and the past is over. Begin anew today…

Be Released from Rage!

WWW (What Went Well)

Use this page to notate what went well as you made practical application of the next steps being RELEASED from RAGE.

Dear...

What would you say if you had to write a note of encouragement to someone who needs to be RELEASED from Rage?

Lest We Forget

Use this section to write a poem or other piece for recitation, compose a song, draw a cartoon, take a photograph and tape it here or any other type of creative expression that will trigger remembrance of the need to remain RELEASED from RAGE.

Purposeful Prayer

Incorporate what you have learned into your daily prayers. Locate relevant scriptures and write them down as you commit them to memory for inclusion in times of prayer.

JEALOUSY & ENVY

Look at the siblings. Are they twins? So very similar yet nuances of difference. They suck from the breast of carnality. A steady always ready diet of pride and selfishness. Swaddle them in the luxurious blanket of vanity. Lay them to nap in the crib of complaint and murmuring. We should refer to them by their proper names lest we forget.

Jealousy and Envy.
Are they twins?

Jealousy

Resentment against a rival, a person enjoying success or advantage , etc or against another's success or advantage itself; Mental uneasiness from suspicion or fear of rivalry, unfaithfulness, etc.
Vigilance in maintaining or guarding something

Envy

A feeling of discontent or covetousness with regard to another's advantages, success, possessions, etc.

Ill will – a feeling of discontent because of another's advantages, possessions, etc., resentful dislike of another who has something that one desires

The main difference between jealousy and envy is that envy is an emotion relating to coveting what someone else has while jealousy is the emotion related to fear that something you have will be taken away by someone else. Envy occurs when we lack a desired attribute enjoyed by another.

Jealousy occurs when something we already possess (usually a special relationship) is threatened by a third person. I want what you have. That is envy. I am afraid that you will take what I already have; that's jealousy. Most people don't actually know the difference between jealousy and envy. They are both rooted in low self-esteem, fear, and a lack of faith in God.

Let me explain. When you are confident in who you are, another's position is of no concern to you. Whether they are smarter, thinner, richer, more popular, a better swimmer, runner or golfer will not cause you one moment of worry. I don't need what you have because what I have is good for me. I know that Jesus sits at the right hand of God the Father and makes intercession for me. I know that I am Hephzibah and that God delights in me. I know that I am the "you" in Jeremiah 29:11, when God says, "I know the plans that I have for you; plans to prosper you and give you a good future."

Is it not true that both envy and jealousy are an affront to the sovereignty of God? We insult God when we look at what someone else has as if what God has given us is somehow inferior. We make light of the power of God when we decide that what someone else has should be ours. Obviously, God has either made a mistake in failing to give this to me or I simply refuse to wait around for God to get this to me.

I know what would be best for me and surely this thing, even though it belongs to someone else, would be best for me – NOW. Additionally, I feel threatened that what I have might be in jeopardy. I will not trust God to protect this thing for me (Note: the thing could be a relationship, position, etc.). I refuse to keep my eyes on God and trust Him. Instead, I will keep my eyes on the one I believe will take what is mine.

Be RELEASED from resentment of rivals, discontent with regards to another's success and the bondage of jealousy and envy. Learn to love God and trust that He knows what you need and will give you your wants as they line up for your good. Trust God!

Jealousy and Envy, be gone!

<u>NEXT STEPS</u>

Have you allowed Jealousy and or Envy to burden you with unnecessary stress? It takes a lot of energy to pay attention to what someone else has, compare it to what you have, decide to take theirs or stay on the lookout lest someone takes yours. That's too much, really. Just stop. Trust God, trust that He loves you and what He has for you is for you. Trust that there is no lack in the Kingdom of God. Trust that God did not and will not run out of blessings. He has enough for you. Jealousy and Envy cause us to lose focus on the true Source of true blessings. There is a hymn which says:

> Turn your eyes upon Jesus
> Look full in His wonderful face
> And the things of Earth will grow strangely dim
> In the light of His glory and grace

Focus on Jesus and watch people and their stuff dim in comparison.

PRACTICAL APPLICATION

Identify one area of your life where you have been walking in
Jealousy and or Envy. Write a letter to God honestly
detailing why you have felt as you have. Remember He is our
Heavenly Father and He longs to hear from us. Be honest
and completely transparent. It's not that He does not already
know, the point is that you must trust Him with your pain.
Today commit to prayerfully confronting Jealousy and Envy
in your life.

Lord, I trust You!

WWW (What Went Well)

Use this page to notate what went well as you made practical application of the next steps being RELEASED from JEALOUSY and ENVY.

Dear...

What would you say if you had to write a note of encouragement to someone who needs to be RELEASED from Jealousy and Envy?

Lest We Forget

Use this section to write a poem or other piece for recitation, compose a song, draw a cartoon, take a photograph and tape it here or any other type of creative expression that will trigger remembrance of the need to remain RELEASED from JEALOUSY and ENVY.

Purposeful Prayer

Incorporate what you have learned into your daily prayers. Locate relevant scriptures and write them down as you commit them to memory for inclusion in times of prayer.

He's smarter

She's wealthier

Bigger house, better car

Greener grass

Colder ice

Fresher air

And then there's me.

Not as bright, rich, or happy.

Apartment, bus pass, no yard

Warm water, polluted air

Yeah, that's me

Low Self-Esteem?

Or

No Self-Esteem

RELEASED!

LOW SELF ESTEEM

Self esteem refers to how a person judges his or her own worth. It is how I view myself, my attitude towards myself. The words "my" and "self" appear a lot. Herein lies the problem with low self esteem. Let me explain. If I view myself as lowly or my attitude towards me is one of low regard then I am said to have "low self esteem." But note that the only opinion that was taken into account was mine or the "my" opinion of "my"self.

I propose that when I only look to me for answers defeat is inevitable. If I look to God to define my worth, then the view changes. Often the lens though which one peers will greatly affect the vision. When I look at myself through God's eyes, I see that I am more than a conqueror (Romans 8:31-39). I see that I am fearfully and wonderfully made according to Psalm 139:14.

> If I look to God to define my worth, then the view changes.

The sin of low self-esteem is that it is really a snubbing of God. It is a rebellion masked in pompous humility. It, at first glance, appears to be humility but in truth it is pride, thinly and cheaply masked. Allow me to clarify... Instead of allowing God to define me as He has already in His word, I define myself. Instead of regarding His view of me as true, I reject God's statement about me and instead adhere to and accept "my" opinion of "myself" even though it is in direct contradiction to what God has and is saying.

To accept "my" opinion as truth instead of God's opinion is Pride. To reject God's opinion and favor your own is to say, "God I am right and You are wrong," God forbid! Yet, when we walk in low self-esteem this is exactly what we do. Recognize it for what it truly is and don't be deceived any longer! What does God say about me? Am I not made in the image of God according to Genesis 1:27? Am I not fearfully and wonderfully made according to Psalm 139:14? The Word of God speaks. He is God and I am not. I view "myself" as He sees me, not as I see myself.

From low self-esteem, I am Released!

NEXT STEPS

Straighten your back and sit up. Come out of the corner and stand up. Get out of the background and come into the foreground. Be honest with yourself about low self-esteem. Have you allowed lies to shape the opinion you have of yourself? God has uniquely gifted you and He is counting on you to obediently fulfill your purpose. Pray and ask God to remove the scales from your eyes and the plugs from your ears. Ask God to reiterate who you are in His sight. Ask God to heal the lies that have kept you in low or no self-esteem. Begin to write down when you first remember feeling inferior. Was a painful word spoken by a parent, sibling or acquaintance? Did a glance in the mirror reveal something different from what was seen in the Fashion Magazine? Did a failed attempt hypnotize you? **Trace It Face It Erase It!** God is not mad at you. The past is over. This is a new day and the Power of God is available because His delight is, always was and always will be in you! You are fearfully and wonderfully made! You can do ALL THINGS through Christ if you would receive the strength that He is offering you. You are RELEASED from Low Self-Esteem.

PRACTICAL APPLICATION

Identify one area of your life where you have allowed Low Self-Esteem to limit your progress. Write down how your movement will be different now that you are RELEASED.

"Our deepest fear is not that we are inadequate. Our deepest fear is that we are powerful beyond measure. It is our light, not our darkness that most frightens us. We ask ourselves, Who am I to be brilliant, gorgeous, talented, fabulous? Actually, who are you *not* to be? You are a child of God. Your playing small does not serve the world. There is nothing enlightened about shrinking so that other people won't feel insecure around you. We are all meant to shine, as children do. We were born to make manifest the glory of God that is within us. It's not just in some of us; it's in everyone. And as we let our own light shine, we unconsciously give other people permission to do the same. As we are liberated from our own fear, our presence automatically liberates others."

Our Deepest Fear by Marianne Williamson

WWW (What Went Well)

Use this page to notate what went well as you made practical application of the next steps being RELEASED from LOW SELF-ESTEEM.

Dear...

What would you say if you had to write a note of encouragement to someone who needs to be RELEASED from Low Self-Esteem?

Lest We Forget

Use this section to write a poem or other piece for recitation, compose a song, draw a cartoon, take a photograph and tape it here or any other type of creative expression that will trigger remembrance of the need to remain RELEASED from LOW SELF-ESTEEM.

Purposeful Prayer

Incorporate what you have learned into your daily prayers. Locate relevant scriptures and write them down as you commit them to memory for inclusion in times of prayer.

Fear the root!

Even though this you cannot see.

Fear the root!

On the surface gentle, kind, and harmless I be.

Fear the root!

Be hypnotized by my beauty, become drunk with my caress

Fear the root!

One day it will be seen, that which is hidden is not less

Fear the root!

Bitterness

BITTERNESS

Bitterness is a root. A root is usually not immediately visible. The root is usually underground, undercover, hidden from everyday sight. You can see the tree but not the root. The tree may be 50 feet tall. You can see the trunk, the leaves, the branches, and the limbs but not the root.

Some roots can grow as deep as the tree is high. The root of bitterness goes deeper and deeper into our spirit as time goes by. What causes this root to come forth?
Usually some act of sin. Abuse in its many forms: sexual, physical mental social, spiritual. Unfulfilled desires which have not been surrendered to God's timing. Social injustices perceived and actual. Deeply held feelings of rejection and low self-esteem. Unrequited love, unfulfilled covenants, this list is massive. The bottom line is that some negative emotion was not surrendered to God

Instead, this negative emotion was allowed to attach itself to the very core of your being like a vine wraps around a water pipe going up a house. It entangles itself and almost becomes a part of you – but it is not. One day it will seek to overtake you. It will control the way you act and react. If you deal with only the surface, that which is easily visible, you've missed it. It will simply resurface because you must get to the root of the problem.

Yes, she is sexually promiscuous but what is the root of the promiscuity? What you can see is merely a symptom of the problem, a branch, a limb but not the root. Perhaps the root is low self-esteem. I need to have a lover whisper sweet nothings to me so I can feel wanted. Perhaps it is pain from past sexual abuse as a child or an adult. Now I see that my body allows me to have power over others. I use my body to control because I will never, ever be the victim again! I hate what happened to me and I will make sure it never happens to me again. I am in control! Yet under the surface is a root of bitterness that has been allowed to gestate deep within your spirit.

To remove the root you must go deep. It will hurt, but once the root is removed, it can never grow back. What root of bitterness is within you? Is it bitterness against the opposite sex? Another race of people? A family or church member? Against yourself? Or is it against God because He allowed that thing to happen?

Fear the root! Face the root!

Surrender the root to the fire of God. Fear can be good when it compels you to take action instead of being complacent and immobile. Fear can cause you to recognize and acknowledge true danger. Don't allow the root to live another day. Submit yourself to God; don't move, allow Him to do a deep work. The fire of God will destroy the root.

Release!

<u>NEXT STEPS</u>

What roots have caused you to become bitter? The root of racism, sexism, classism? You must **Trace It Face It Erase It.** When did the root begin? Remember the root is deep, probably deeper than you realize. Roots tend to be expansive. This kind will only come out by fasting and prayer according to Matthew 17:21. You must pray and ask God to reveal the root of the bitterness. You may even have to pray and ask God to reveal actual areas in which we have become bitter. Often we have been bitter for so long we don't even classify it as actual bitterness. "It is what it is and I just deal with it" "I am a realist that's all" "If I don't have any expectations I will never be disappointed" The root is deep but you can and will experience RELEASE.

To remove the root you must go deep. It will hurt, but once the root is removed, it can never grow back. Jasina B. Wise

PRACTICAL APPLICATION

Identify an area of your life where you have become bitter.
This will be painful. It will require honest introspection,
prayer and fasting. Pray before you write in your journal. Ask
God to provide revelation and deliverance. Anytime a root is
removed from the ground it is messy. Don't be tempted to
accept removal of only a portion of the root. Persevere until
the entire root is removed. If a trace of the root is left it can
grow again.

WWW (What Went Well)

Use this page to notate what went well as you made practical application of the next steps being RELEASED from BITTNERNESS.

Dear...

What would you say if you had to write a note of encouragement to someone who needs to be RELEASED from Bitterness?

<u>Lest We Forget</u>

Use this section to write a poem or other piece for recitation, compose a song, draw a cartoon, take a photograph and tape it here or any other type of creative expression that will trigger remembrance of the need to remain RELEASED from BITTERNESS.

Purposeful Prayer

Incorporate what you have learned into your daily prayers. Locate relevant scriptures and write them down as you commit them to memory for inclusion in times of prayer.

He said what? She said What?

She did what? With who? When?

Don't say I said and you didn't hear it from me BUT –

Now you know I'm not one to gossip…

GOSSIP

Thou shall not kill. Yet we think nothing of killing another's reputation by repeating unconfirmed details. Isn't it interesting how people try to clean up the dirt. Unconfirmed details, why not just call it what it is? Gossip.
The release comes in two forms, release from gossiping and release from allowing gossip to affect you. In other words, don't gossip about others and don't allow the gossip of others to negatively impact you.

There is nothing innocent about gossip. It is mean spirited and indicative of spiritual immaturity. The same person who would be appalled at the thought of picking up a knife and slicing the throat of another human being will casually engage in "juicy gossip." The results are the same. Death.

> Gossip kills. It is neither innocent, sexy, nor cute. It is, in fact, malicious, repugnant, and satanic.

The death of another's reputation, influence, respect, privacy, trust, etc. Gossip kills. It is neither innocent, sexy, nor cute. It is, in fact, malicious, repugnant, and satanic. The release from the affect of gossip requires that you know who you are in Christ. Who does Christ say that you are? What does God say that you can do and have? When you are confident in the fact that you are more than a conquerer you don't concern yourself with what others say about you. You must know that your hope is built on nothing less than Jesus and HIS righteousness.

Only God has the power to define you. What man thinks of me is irrelevant. I am on this earth to fulfill the will of my Father. I, you, we, cannot allow ourselves to be distracted from our assignment. We are, like Jesus, to do the will of our Father, God.

NEXT STEPS

Gossip is lethal. It can bring death whether you are the one gossiping or the one being gossiped about. Death of trust, death of character, death of fellowship, death of confidence. You shall not Murder, surely the taking of life in any form is Murder. The life or vitality of trust, character, fellowship or confidence. Have you participated in gossip? Did you initiate or simply participate? Either way, Repent. Ask God to forgive you for participating in any way.

Have you been the victim of gossip? You are RELEASED from the negative effects of Gossip! Pray for the person/people who gossiped about you. Pray for them and forgive them. (..For they know not what they do)

PRACTICAL APPLICATION

For the next 21 days journal about the powerful effect of "words". Write about how words have affected you over the years. Take note of the words that you use when talking to those close to you. Do your words build up or tear down? If they tear down begin to retrain yourself to speak words that are affirming. Whether speaking about others or yourself, we must learn to speak words that affirm and not slay.

But the human tongue can be tamed by no man. It is a restless (undisciplined, irreconcilable) evil, full of deadly poison. With it we bless the Lord and Father, and with it we curse men who were made in God's likeness! Out of the same mouth come forth blessing and cursing. These things, my brethren, ought not to be so. Does a fountain send forth [simultaneously] from the same opening fresh water and bitter?
(James 3:8-11 Amplified Bible)

<u>WWW (What Went Well)</u>

Use this page to notate what went well as you made practical application of the next steps being RELEASED from GOSSIP.

Dear...

What would you say if you had to write a note of encouragement to someone who needs to be RELEASED from Gossip?

Lest We Forget

Use this section to write a poem or other piece for recitation, compose a song, draw a cartoon, take a photograph and tape it here or any other type of creative expression that will trigger remembrance of the need to remain RELEASED from GOSSIP.

Purposeful Prayer

Incorporate what you have learned into your daily prayers. Locate relevant scriptures and write them down as you commit them to memory for inclusion in times of prayer.

If I was smarter

If I was thinner

If I was prettier

If I was richer

If I was taller

If I could play ball

If I could cook

If I could run faster

If I could swim farther

If I could dance better

If I was, If I could

They would like me, love me, include me, invite me, marry me, pick me,

"Me!" Wait…who is "**Me**?"

PEOPLE PLEASER

The bad thing about trying to please people is that you usually end up displeasing yourself. Why is it that my need to please you causes me to compromise my wants and desires? I tend to compromise who I truly am as I seek to gain your approval. When did the creation become master? Why do I elevate other people to a level that only God should occupy? My desire should be to please God in everything I do.

As I do so everyone who is in the correct God ordained space in my life will be pleased (according to God's perfect will). I am not speaking of a healthy desire to do what is right and please those with whom you are in legitimate relationship. I am referring to the unhealthy preoccupation with seeking the approval of people that God never told you to commune so closely with.

Trying to please everyone is exhausting. STOP!

We make things difficult but the solution really is simple.

STOP!

NEXT STEPS

Be honest, who have you really been trying to please? Is it a neighbor, a potential spouse, the in-crowd at school, an in-law? Begin to question yourself about why you are making certain decisions. What is your true motivation? Is it merely to get the promotion or because it is the Godly thing to do? The fact that it will get the promotion is just a byproduct of obedience to God. (Godly obedience does have its perks ☺) This is going to take some brutal honesty because the only one who can really answer the question about true intentions is YOU. Now we know that God knows, He is omniscient. Those around you can only guess and suppose, but you know. Even if you won't admit it to anyone else, to thine own self be true, if you have been doing things merely to please people-Stop. Who do you love the most? Who is the One you want to please the most?

PRACTICAL APPLICATION

Identify one area in which you are guilty of being a People Pleaser. Has it been at Church, at work, at your child's school, at the hair salon, with the college friends or with your distant relatives? Pray and ask God what His desire is for you in that area. Begin today to start modifying your behavior to align with what will please God instead of what will be simply impressive to people. Start with one area and spread your new found freedom to other areas. Today you are RELEASED from being a People Pleaser!

Too many people spend money they haven't earned, to buy things they don't want, to impress people they don't like. (Will Rogers)

WWW (What Went Well)

Use this page to notate what went well as you made practical application of the next steps being RELEASED from being a PEOPLE PLEASER.

Dear...

What would you say if you had to write a note of encouragement to someone who needs to be RELEASED from being a People Pleaser?

Lest We Forget

Use this section to write a poem or other piece for recitation, compose a song, draw a cartoon, take a photograph and tape it here or any other type of creative expression that will trigger remembrance of the need to remain RELEASED from being a PEOPLE PLEASER.

Purposeful Prayer

Incorporate what you have learned into your daily prayers. Locate relevant scriptures and write them down as you commit them to memory for inclusion in times of prayer.

Smooth talk

Slow walk

Looks too good to be true

No need to check the facts

No need to verify

Smoking mirrors

Slight of hand

Big bad wolf or simply an innocent puppy in need of love

Shell game

Bait and switch

Released.

Gullible no more.

GULLIBLE

Children are naturally gullible. Easily fooled, quick to believe the untrue. We excuse the gullibility of a child. They are inexperienced and have not yet lived long enough to know better. They are innocent and must be protected. It's okay in a child but unacceptable in an adult. The exception must be made for adults who are developmentally or otherwise medically challenged. In fact, gullibility can be a medical symptom of not typically developed individuals. I am speaking to those who do not fall into that category. I am speaking to the typically developing majority. It is time to be RELEASED from being gullible.

Stop allowing yourself to be tricked and manipulated. Start checking stories. Verify things. If you feel like something is wrong, pray! As a matter of fact, pray before you think something is wrong. Stop making decisions in a vacuum. Seek the opinion of other godly level-headed people. Remember some of the stuff the old folks said. Yes, some of it was crazy but most of it was sound wisdom!

If it walks like a dog and barks like a dog then don't get mad when the dog bites you! A dog that will bring a bone will carry one too. Fool me once, shame on you. Fool me twice, shame on me. A fool and his money are soon parted.

Don't let what your partner brings to the table be the only thing you have to eat. Why buy the cow if you can get the milk for free.

Ain't nothing common about sense.

Stop allowing emotions like desperation to rule you. Use your brain. Pray and ask God to give you wisdom. Get rid of silly immature people in your close circle of friends. They can be associates but don't get advice from them and don't allow them to get too close to you. Why? Because stupidity is contagious.

NEXT STEPS

Sometimes we can want something so badly that we don't want to hear truth which may show that it is not good for us. Sometimes we just don't want to put in the work that is needed to verify facts. It is so much easier to sit back and trust that others have confirmed truth. Sometimes we don't want to discipline ourselves in prayer to seek the truth from God. We don't want to search God's Word for truth, for that would require effort. Does any of this resonate with you? If you see a pattern of being misled or continuous episodes of believing lies, you need to be Released from being Gullible.

You were not created to be constantly misled. You have access to the Creator of the Universe and He will show you things which previously were unknown to you. (Jer. 33:3). Stop expecting everyone else to confirm the facts for you, confirm for yourself. When you were a young child your guardians were charged to validate for you. You are no longer a young child; you must develop the maturity to shield yourself from unscrupulous people who prey on the gullible.

Identify specific instances where you were deceived. Evaluate the episode paying close attention to how the truth was able to be hidden from you. Did you fail to pray? Did you make a major decision without consulting Godly counsel? Did you disregard the advice of Godly counsel? What reoccurring patterns in your behavior do you see?

PRACTICAL APPLICATION

In the Next Steps you identified areas were you were
previously Gullible. You also identified specific patterns in
your own behavior that make you susceptible to those who
prey on the Gullible. Pray and ask God to give you wisdom.
Pray and ask God to reveal any people in your life who are
or have taken advantage of you. You must ask God for
strength to remove those people and or situations from your
life. Ask God to forgive you for not asking for wisdom
sooner, but acknowledge that you are now ready to receive
wisdom and act upon it. You are RELEASED from being
Gullible. Stay free!

As a dog returns to its vomit, so a fool repeats his
foolishness (Proverbs 26:11 NKJV)

WWW (What Went Well)

Use this page to notate what went well as you made practical application of the next steps being RELEASED from being GULLIBLE.

Dear...

What would you say if you had to write a note of encouragement to someone who needs to be RELEASED from being Gullible?

<u>Lest We Forget</u>

Use this section to write a poem or other piece for recitation, compose a song, draw a cartoon, take a photograph and tape it here or any other type of creative expression that will trigger remembrance of the need to remain RELEASED from being GULLIBLE.

Purposeful Prayer

Incorporate what you have learned into your daily prayers. Locate relevant scriptures and write them down as you commit them to memory for inclusion in times of prayer.

Just enough is good enough

Too much is just too much

Not too hot, not too cold

Not too young, not too old

Not too rich, not too poor

Not through the window

Not through the door

I will stay here

Never move forward

Never go back

No to abundance

No to lack

On the surface it sounds good but don't be no fool

I must be RELEASED.

Mediocrity is not cool!

MEDIOCRITY

> We insult the greatness that God has placed within each of us when we settle.

Mediocrity is accepting average. It is stopping at ordinary and not even attempting greatness. We must be delivered from the spirit of mediocrity.

Doing just enough to get by. Accepting less than greatness from ourselves. Past failed attempts can cause us to accept mediocrity. "Oh well, at least I have somebody (or someone)." "It's ok; this is good enough." Why settle? Why settle for good enough without even striving for more? We insult the greatness that God has placed within each of us when we settle. Never settle for less than what God has said is possible. God said in His Word that we are the head and not the tail, above and not beneath (Deuteronomy 28:13).

The promise is of course contingent upon obedience to God. Yet those of us who are walking in obedience and repentance still allow the spirit of mediocrity to limit us. Be released. This is not your portion! It is logical that if you have failed continuously you will eventually expect failure. We don't live by mere logic; we live by faith in God. It matters not what has happened before. God has said that I will triumph. Therefore, I will not stop until I have triumphed. I will not accept a half victory. Average and ordinary do not describe Jehovah or His works. He has done marvelous things. He is great! His promises to me are great (2 Peter 1:4).

Why do I limit my expectation of Him (and that which He has created, me)? You must expect great things. This is faith put in action. Do not allow the enemy to seduce you into thinking that ordinary is all there is. The father of lies continues to birth untruth. God wants you to excel. God's nature is excellence and we are His children. We have His DNA. Genetically we have strands of His greatness woven into our very essence. Be released from the ordinary. Reject the average. Believe God! Trust that God is able to do exceeding, abundantly, above all that you can even imagine. Over are all the days of just barely getting by. From this day forward determine to accept nothing less than God's very best!

NEXT STEPS

Take a moment and be completely honest with yourself. Identify one area of your life in which you have settled. You know what your original dreams were. You may have halted your pursuit because of dwindling finances, lack of family support, adverse physical health, advanced age, or any other myriad of factors. You are RELEASED. You are no longer going to accept mediocrity from yourself. You will excel with this task. Don't accept less than complete fulfillment. You can do this. You are starting with just one area. Don't get overwhelmed with the magnitude of multiple areas. Your focus is just one area for now. You must change your expectation. Expect to succeed. Pray and ask God to heal you from whatever caused you to be susceptible to mediocrity. There will always be a root. The root must be destroyed by prayer, faith and pursuit. Pray and ask for God's help. Have faith that God is willing and able to help you. Passionately pursue the prize. Don't stop mid-lap, finish the race. It doesn't matter in which place you finish, just finish.

PRACTICAL APPLICATION

Mediocrity is a sin because at its core is an expression of rebellion against the Word of God. Deuteronomy 28:13 proclaims us to be the head and not the tail, above and not beneath. God's expectation of us is excellence, when we settle for less we are rejecting God's expectation. This is rebellion. For the next 21 days identify one area that you have settled in, commit to pray and journal about God's direction for you in this particular area. During this period, whatever God tells you to do, do it. You will receive fresh revelation and direction. God is a restorer of life. He will breathe new life into this area.

I know your [record of] works *and* what you are doing; you are neither cold nor hot. Would that you were cold or hot! So, because you are lukewarm and neither cold nor hot, I will spew you out of My mouth! (Revelation 3:15-16 Amplified Bible)

WWW (What Went Well)

Use this page to notate what went well as you made practical application of the next steps being RELEASED from MEDIOCRITY.

Dear...

What would you say if you had to write a note of encouragement to someone who needs to be RELEASED from Mediocrity?

Lest We Forget

Use this section to write a poem or other piece for recitation, compose a song, draw a cartoon, take a photograph and tape it here or any other type of creative expression that will trigger remembrance of the need to remain RELEASED from MEDIOCRITY.

Purposeful Prayer

Incorporate what you have learned into your daily prayers. Locate relevant scriptures and write them down as you commit them to memory for inclusion in times of prayer.

Pull down the shades

Don't turn on the light

I can barely move

What's the point?

I don't feel like it

I don't want to

I can't move

I am not interested

Just go without me

I am going to snuggle with my new best friend

Lethargy

LETHARGY

Lethargy is lack of energy and enthusiasm. Feeling like a slug (you know that shell-less cousin to the snail). Just barely moving along. Always coming up on the "rough side of the mountain." Jesus did not die so that you could just barely make it all the time.

> Lethargy is rooted in weakness. What or who has stolen your strength?

Lethargy is rooted in weakness. What or who has stolen your strength? Hope deferred makes the heart sick according to Proverbs 13:12. Have unfilled desires or delayed miracles caused you to become tired? Has the wait worn you out, worn you down? Have repeated disappointments caused you to surrender and retreat into mere existence? Has the thief who comes but to steal, kill and destroy, stolen your joy, killed your zest for life, and destroyed your optimism? Be RELEASED!

There is a season for all things. Lethargy bespeaks of a season that has lingered too long. You cannot wallow in sorrow, disappointment, or any other negative emotion. Wipe your tears, breathe, and get up! Get up and get on with your life.

Lethargy means you are stuck. You have allowed whatever or whomever to cage you into a catatonic state of mere existence. This state brings no glory to God. We must rise above, break out and allow our lives to be a testimony to the restorative power of Christ Jesus!

Allow the Holy Spirit to infuse you with a heavenly dose of B12. You have no strength because you have no joy. The joy of the Lord is your strength. Learn to laugh. Laugh at yourself and others. Smile sometimes. Your face won't crack (unless you have obsessed on plastic surgeries or botox – smile). How hard was that? You actually smiled.

As long as you are alive you are a candidate for God's blessings and miracles. Pray to God. Give your life to Him. Believe in Him and expect Him to bless you.

Repeat after me...In the name of Jesus, I am RELEASED from Lethargy! Amen

NEXT STEPS

There is a legitimate need for rest. Lethargy does not address a legitimate need. No, lethargy is a response to spiritual depletion. We have already addressed the fact that the joy of the Lord is your strength. If you are feeling completely depleted of all energy and strength you have been robbed! Who or what has stolen your joy? Identify the thief; was it someone or something from within or without? Did an external force cause you to internally concede defeat? Did an internal force manifest in external concessions of defeat? Get up! It was not said of you that "upon thy belly shalt thou go, and dust shalt thou eat all the days of thy life:" (Gen 3:14 KJV). You were created to "sit in heavenly places" (Ephesians 2:6). Turn your eyes toward Heaven and refocus.

PRACTICAL APPLICATION

The joy of the Lord is your strength! Start reading scriptures that celebrate the goodness of God. Read positive testimonies that affirm the power of God. Begin to recount times in your life when God healed your body or answered your prayer. Sing songs to God about His greatness and how much you love Him. The songs can even be originals from your heart to God. (It doesn't matter if you are a skilled singer or not, this song is only meant for the ears of your Heavenly Father. He loves the sound of your voice because He created you and loves you with an everlasting love!) Distance yourself from negative people who want to wallow in self-pity and the "woe is me(s)". Surround yourself with people who accentuate the positive and eliminate the negative. Choose joy. Choose to be RELEASED!

We must rise above, break out and allow our lives to be a testimony to the restorative power of Christ Jesus!

Jasina B. Wise

WWW (What Went Well)

Use this page to notate what went well as you made practical application of the next steps being RELEASED from LETHARGY.

Dear...

What would you say if you had to write a note of encouragement to someone who needs to be RELEASED from Lethargy?

Lest We Forget

Use this section to write a poem or other piece for recitation, compose a song, draw a cartoon, take a photograph and tape it here or any other type of creative expression that will trigger remembrance of the need to remain RELEASED from LETHARGY.

Purposeful Prayer

Incorporate what you have learned into your daily prayers. Locate relevant scriptures and write them down as you commit them to memory for inclusion in times of prayer.

Crowded room

Music played loud

To be in it but not of it

Outside looking in or inside looking out

Physical pain or mental pause

Crowded room

I am invisible

Music played loud

I do not exist

I am not here

I am…NOT

Screaming, Yelling, Silence

Loneliness.

RELEASED

LONELINESS

Loneliness is social isolation, the emotional response to a
lack of meaningful companionship. Many confuse loneliness
with being alone. They are not the same. To be alone is
sometimes preferred. There may be times when we choose
to be alone or by one's self. I choose to remove myself from
the presence of others. It is an act of my will. I am in
essence in control because I can dictate the start and finish
of the period. I am neither surprised nor overwhelmed.

But loneliness is different. Loneliness is seemingly beyond
my control. Loneliness somehow
personifies into an entity that
supersedes my will. In a large
crowded room, loneliness will
appear and cause one to see, hear,
and be aware of the presence of
others yet perceive solitude.

> Trace it.
>
> Face it.
>
> Erase it.

The perception becomes more
valid than reality. To combat this we must trace it to the
root. The root was created when certain things were allowed
to germinate. That which was initially small was allowed to
expand into something greater. The thought of low self-
esteem, abandonment, fear, unforgiveness, etc. What began
as a small feeling or even thought was never properly dealt
with.

Trace it. Face it. Erase it.

The TFE method forces one to identify the beginning, confront the cause and effect, then nullify the illegitimate power. The nullification occurs through prayer and the power of God. One must not ignore recurrent negative emotions. Immediately confront them in prayer. Do not allow germination to occur. Any weed can be destroyed at the root.

Be RELEASED from Loneliness!

NEXT STEPS

Loneliness is a state that can render even the most seemingly social person an outcast in her mind. Loneliness can make you feel like you are outside in the cold peering into the window of a house where the most glorious party is occurring. You can see the warm fireplace, all of the smiling happy people dressed in bright festive attire as they sample delicious looking foods served on silver platters. You can hear the music through the glass; you can almost feel the warmth from the fire and the lights - but not quite. You are on the other side of the glass and no one sees you. You must make the move to enter the house. Stop lying to yourself and saying that you don't want to be a part of the festivities. You actually do. Stop being afraid of what might happen to you if you go inside. You will never know what good thing could happen until you go inside. You must be honest with yourself and fight your way out of this. The reality is that even though you felt like you were on the outside looking in, loneliness is an area of confinement. You were actually on the inside looking out and you must be RELEASED.

PRACTICAL APPLICATION

Trace It, Face It and Erase It is a method used to combat areas of emotional bondage. Trace the root of the bondage. In this instance the question is where did the feelings of loneliness originate? You may need to pray and ask God to reveal some of the "hidden things" from your past. Sometimes we chose not to remember things that are painful, but the memories are still operating behind the scenes. Prayer and journaling will assist in the tracing of the root. Next we must Face It. Face the reality that whatever happened did indeed happen and that it is now affecting your present and will affect your future if you don't handle it now. I think the most insidious lie that we tell ourselves is "I'm okay". In the words of Shakespeare, "To thine own self be true". It does matter and it can be addressed if you would only face it head on. Next is Erase It. There is no magic eraser, there is Prayer and it is enough. God loves you, He is not mad at you and He can fix what is wrong. God has not forgotten about you. Pray and believe that God loves you. He does indeed love you just as you are today. He is able to give you a better today even if it means healing you from the negative effect of yesterday. You will find yourself no longer feeling lonely. You will not be on the outside looking in or on the inside looking out. You will experience the love of Jesus which will complete you in every area.

[4] Yea, though I walk through the valley of the shadow of death, I will fear no evil; For You *are* with me; Your rod and Your staff, they comfort me. Psalm 23:4(NKJV)

WWW (What Went Well)

Use this page to notate what went well as you made practical application of the next steps being RELEASED from LONELINESS.

<u>Dear...</u>

<u>What would you say if you had to write a note of encouragement to someone who needs to be RELEASED from Loneliness?</u>

Lest We Forget

Use this section to write a poem or other piece for recitation, compose a song, draw a cartoon, take a photograph and tape it here or any other type of creative expression that will trigger remembrance of the need to remain RELEASED from LONELINESS.

Purposeful Prayer

Incorporate what you have learned into your daily prayers. Locate relevant scriptures and write them down as you commit them to memory for inclusion in times of prayer.

I want it

No, I must have it

I will die if I don't get it.

No, I don't want to live if I can't have it!

Enslaving desire

Confining passion

Inclination

Impulse

Wanting, Wishing, Blinding, Binding

All consuming asphyxiation

Mind controlling dedication

Lest. I. Die!

RELEASE LUST

LUST

Lust is extreme want. It is a want which defines, directs, and controls. A lust for knowledge can be a good thing in theory, however lust always seems to distort that which could have been good. It is the extreme nature of lust which causes the transition from good to evil.

Lust causes the desire to become all consuming. Lust usually carries a negative connotation. This is that from which we must be released. That negative quicksand of obsessive, desperate hunger which controls to the point that we will do absolutely anything to achieve fulfillment.

Lust is an exercise of extremes. I can wish to obtain a position of power because I legitimately want to influence positive change.

Lust is an exercise of extremes. I can wish to obtain a position of power because I legitimately want to influence positive change. Yet, when I lust for power to the point that I am willing to compromise myself and others, the extreme has overpowered my initial good intentions. At this point, I am on the proverbial path to hell which is always freshly paved with "good intentions." It is not wrong to desire riches to help others. To be in a position to care for your family and others is admirable. Financial stability is a positive thing; however, when the desire is taken to the extreme the collateral damage is anything but positive.

Suppose I become so fixated on my desire for wealth that I will do anything to get it. I begin to compromise God's laws, my family and my integrity. Nothing is off limits to be sacrificed on the altar of my fixated lust. The seed has grown awry. The problem can only be permanently destroyed at the root. The question can be asked, "How can I stop this process before it occurs?" The answer is simple, Prayer. Submit every desire to God in prayer. Pray daily that God will direct you. Ask God to examine your heart and keep your motives pure. Seek godly, mature counsel from those who will not give you the answers you want, but the truth without compromise.

This will address prevention but how do you confront lust which has already germinated? Again, prayer, but also repentance which involves a change in actions. Pray for God to reveal the true magnitude of the problem (remember most roots are underground and are usually deeper and more far reaching than one would think). Pray for God to perform a change of heart and mind. Pray for God to touch the hearts of those who have been negatively impacted by the selfish pursuit. Pray that relationships will be healed. Most importantly, pray that God will forgive the sin of lust and that permanent change will ensue. Lastly, commit to daily declarations thanking God that you are forvever RELEASED from lust.

NEXT STEPS

Remember that extreme want can be channeled to the positive or negative. Earlier a "lust" for knowledge was referenced. This can be good right? Well with most things it can go either way. A sincere desire for information without restraint is wrong. You are not justified by the end if the means violated another's legitimate rights. The Word of God is the best filter. It's usually less about what you did but more about how you did it. Lust is extreme. It loses sight of everything and everyone else. Lust is concerned with fulfillment. It gives no thought to the residual effects. Lust is the monstrosity of a desire. What is the filter for your desires? Examine yourself. What have you sacrificed in your pursuit? Some sacrifices are legitimate, delayed gratification is actually a sign of mature decision making. Lust is completely different; it gives no thought at all to delay or denial of other wants. Lust dismisses all but its intended target. Have you dismissed legitimate relationships? Have you compromised who God created you to be? When it began you were in control of the desire but really, what is in control now? Is the pursuit controlling you? Have you traded God being in control of your life for your life being controlled by this desire? Do you even seek God's direction anymore or are you simply guided by this pursuit?

PRACTICAL APPLICATION

Identify the area where lust has taken root. Pray, ask God to forgive you and heal you. Ask God to heal others who have been injured by the lust in your life. Ask God to provide restoration. Ask God to provide you with an accountability partner; a person who will walk with you in honesty and integrity. An accountability partner will not be afraid to confront you in love when needed. This person will be a mature person of prayer and wisdom. (Only God can reveal that about a person-don't trust what you think you see or know!) You were RELEASED from lust the moment you prayed with a sincere heart. I now charge you to walk in your freedom!

Lord, examine my heart and keep my motives pure.

WWW (What Went Well)

Use this page to notate what went well as you made practical application of the next steps being RELEASED from LUST.

Dear...

What would you say if you had to write a note of encouragement to someone who needs to be RELEASED from Lust?

<u>Lest We Forget</u>

Use this section to write a poem or other piece for recitation, compose a song, draw a cartoon, take a photograph and tape it here or any other type of creative expression that will trigger remembrance of the need to remain RELEASED from LUST.

Purposeful Prayer

Incorporate what you have learned into your daily prayers. Locate relevant scriptures and write them down as you commit them to memory for inclusion in times of prayer.

You are bad.

I know.

What you did was bad.

I know.

You come from a bad family.

I know.

You have bad friends.

I know.

You look bad. You talk bad. You walk bad. Bad in the morning. Bad in the noon. Bad all night. Not even a good example of bad, actually a pitifully bad example of bad.

…..How can I change?

Silence.

Be RELEASED from condemnation.

CONDEMNATION

Condemnation is a strong disapproval. It is being reminded of your failures and shortcomings. Condemnation is the assertion of failure without the offering of solution. People will often mistake condemnation for conviction. Conviction is legitimate sorrow and acceptance of God's forgiveness. The difference is that conviction offers a solution and is a tool for positive growth. Condemnation offers no solution and is meant to tear down, debilitate, and ultimately destroy.

Romans 8:1 tells us that there is no condemnation in Christ Jesus. Condemnation is from the devil, not God. You must differentiate between conviction, which offers a solution from God, through the blood of Jesus Christ, and condemnation, which is meant to tear you down with no hope of rebuilding.

Condemnation is an illegitimate attack meant to mortally wound you. Reject condemnation! Do not allow condemning thoughts to linger. Combat condemnation with the Word of God. John 1:9 says, "If we confess our sins, He is faithful and just to forgive us our sins, and to cleanse us from all unrighteousness." You do not have to deny the reality of any situation, but Jesus has offered forgiveness for all of your wrongs. Jesus is more powerful than my "bad." I do not need to wallow in any situation. I repent, accept forgiveness, and keep moving forward. Be RELEASED from condemnation!

NEXT STEPS

Some people like to live in your past; usually these are the same people who have selective memory with matters of their own past wrongs. Pray for these people but limit your contact with them. Reflection of past events can be a healthy exercise when information is gathered that will prevent future mistakes. Reflection in this instance is specifically targeted at positive behavior modification. Reflection which does not offer solution is counter-productive and sometimes destructive. Don't entertain thoughts that cause you to think less of yourself. Do not accept this from others about you or from yourself about you. If you are left feeling depressed and minimalized – it was probably condemnation. Were positive solutions offered? Was authentic prayer offered? Do not accept condemnation. Reject it and the carrier. If they are being carried from the enemy in your mind; reject those thoughts. If they are from someone else, reject those words that were meant to hurt and weaken you. You are who God says you are. You are what God says you are. God says that you are **Forgiven.** Right now, you are RELEASED from condemnation!

PRACTICAL APPLICATION

In every area that you have allowed condemnation to fester, end it right now! When do the thoughts usually come to you? Is there a particular time of night or day? Is it when you are physically tired or emotionally drained? Is there a certain person who always seems to sprinkle a dash of condemnation into every conversation? Is there a particular group gathering that leaves you feeling condemned, confused and isolated? Pray and ask God to reveal the truth. Begin to write down how you feel after these toxic encounters. Insanity is doing the same thing but expecting different results. Stop allowing hurtful people access to you. Stop entertaining condemning thoughts. The enemy only comes to kill you- physically, emotionally and or spiritually. Furthermore he wants to destroy the good progress that you have made by God's grace. And without a doubt he wants to steal your joy by sending distraction and emotional intimidation. Condemnation is one of his munitions of choice. Fear not, no weapon formed against you shall proper! You are RELEASED from condemnation!

WWW (What Went Well)

Use this page to notate what went well as you made practical application of the next steps being RELEASED from CONDEMNATION.

<u>Dear...</u>

<u>*What would you say if you had to write a note of encouragement to someone who needs to be RELEASED from Condemnation?*</u>

<u>Lest We Forget</u>

Use this section to write a poem or other piece for recitation, compose a song, draw a cartoon, take a photograph and tape it here or any other type of creative expression that will trigger remembrance of the need to remain RELEASED from CONDEMNATION.

Purposeful Prayer

Incorporate what you have learned into your daily prayers. Locate relevant scriptures and write them down as you commit them to memory for inclusion in times of prayer.

Shades of blue overwhelm me...

In blue water, I drown.

In blue air I gag.

Shades of grey disarm me...

In gray fog I am blinded.

In gray steel I am entombed.

The room is gray.

I will never escape shades of blue and gray.

Can you hear my cries for help?

I need a champion. I need to be RELEASED from depression and hopelessness.

Now!

DEPRESSION AND HOPELESSNESS

Depression and hopelessness are the result of sustained disappointment, failure, and fear. Proverbs 13:12 references delayed hope or a state of hopelessness making the heart sick. Being without hope or being in a state of hopelessness can lead to depression.

Some people become immobilized by depression and hopelessness. The two become the structure which supports an area of confinement, a room if you may, no, more like a cell. Depression on the left. Hopelessness on the right. Hopelessness above and depression beneath. Encasing, entombing, confining, limiting, and binding. Though these two are emotional, they can also manifest physical symptoms.

Depression can actually feel like a physical ache in your body, wearing a lead suit, cement shoes or a steel hat. It can manifest as pressure and pain in your stomach, legs or arms. Depression and hopelessness are not to be taken "lightly." Sorrow is appropriate in some situations. Yet, a deeper sinister seed can begin to form if sorrow is not submitted to God in prayer. Without prayer, sorrow morphs into depression or hopelessness.

You must disclose the reason for your sorrow to God. You must have faith to believe that God is able to transform the sorrowful situation into one of victory. You must not entertain negative mental or physical conversations. Reject negativity whenever, wherever, and by whomever. Simply refuse to entertain any knowledge which is contrary to the Word of God.

To do this, you must read the Word of God. In this day and age, you can have the Word of God read to you. You can listen by CD, DVD, MP3's, websites, and smartphones. You must combat the demonic duo of depression and hopelessness with the divine duo of prayer and the Word of God. Pray for God to reveal His Word to you. Pray for your faith in God to rise. Rid yourself of negative people, actions, and thoughts.

Be proactive in the search for affirming people, situations, and experiences. Do not wallow, be willing to allow God to change your perspective and confession. Speak out loud and declare the opposite of depression and hopelessness. Affirm that you have the joy of Jesus which is not predicated on current circumstances.

> You must have faith to believe that God is able to transform the sorrowful situation into one of victory.

The joy of Jesus rests solely on the fact that God is sovereign and He is aware of my current state. He is aware; He loves me and He will provide for me. I am not depressed; I am joyful in Jesus! I am not hopeless; I am full of hope. My hope is built on nothing less than Jesus blood and His righteousness. My hope is not dependent on my current circumstances. My hope is not determined by my degree of current success or defeat. My hope is not and never was in myself, another human being, a relationship, an institution, a possession, or a worldly attainment. All of those things are subject to failure and change. My hope is dependent on God alone. God is sovereign. God is omnipotent. God is constant and stable. I have hope! Be RELEASED from depression and hopelessness!

NEXT STEPS

You must believe again. You must believe that God loves you and that God will move on your behalf. This is not a passive statement of universal truth. You must get radical and fight for your life! Depression and hopelessness can lead you to places of no return, places of no physical return and places of no mental return. God is not mad at you; there is nothing that you have ever done that will cause God to stop loving you. You must fight but the weapons of this battle are not what you would expect. You must arm yourself with the Word of God. The promises of God contained in His Word must become like food to you. Depression and Hopelessness are treacherous shadows; they will seek to occupy every inch of your existence. Like a tick full to the point of bursting, they will seek to overshadow everything else in your life. Their intent is to block you from seeing anything or anybody else, especially God. Please recognize how imperative it is that you fight! You matter, your life matters! You have a Champion and His name is Jesus. He loves you so much that He died for you and His love has nothing to do with what you have or have not done. He loves you because He loves you and that fact will never change. He will join you in the fight, He will be your strength. Be RELEASED!

PRACTICAL APPLICATION

You must remove depression and hopelessness from every area of your life. Your thoughts, your words and your deeds must align with the Word of God. No more depressing conversations. No more thoughts of "woe is me". No more acting out of desperation. Read the Bible and make note of scriptures that speak of depression and hopelessness, there are many. Monitor the music that you listen to and movies you watch. No more songs about pathetically pitiful situations and people. No more movies that leave you in a ball of negative emotions. Limit your time with negative people. If depression and hopelessness are areas of bondage in your life, you must guard your freedom. Share this chapter with the negative people but they must work through it on their own-them and Jesus. You will jeopardize your freedom by spending too much time with them. After you have been RELEASED pray and ask God to show you how to help those close to you. Give them a copy of this book and share your personal story of release.

Why are you cast down, O my inner self? And why should you moan over me *and* be disquieted within me? Hope in God *and* wait expectantly for Him, for I shall yet praise Him, Who is the help of my countenance, and my God. (Psalms 42:11 AMP)

WWW (What Went Well)

Use this page to notate what went well as you made practical application of the next steps being RELEASED from DEPRESSION AND HOPELESSNESS.

Dear...

What would you say if you had to write a note of encouragement to someone who needs to be RELEASED from Depression and Hopelessness?

Lest We Forget

Use this section to write a poem or other piece for recitation, compose a song, draw a cartoon, take a photograph and tape it here or any other type of creative expression that will trigger remembrance of the need to remain RELEASED from DEPRESSION and HOPELESSNESS.

Purposeful Prayer

Incorporate what you have learned into your daily prayers. Locate relevant scriptures and write them down as you commit them to memory for inclusion in times of prayer.

To take a gift I did not give

To reject a prize offered in love

To choose the darkness instead of light

To concede defeat when another offered to fight

To silence a voice that needed to be heard

To limit potential, the unspoken word

To never step on the path which will someday lead to a win

To declare an ending when it only did just begin

Be RELEASED from thoughts of suicide

THOUGHTS OF SUICIDE

The enemy comes to steal, kill, and destroy. His ultimate goal is to separate you from eternal life with Jesus Christ. His goal is to cause eternal separation from God Almighty. Understand that the enemy's eternal fate has already been established. He willingly chose eternal separation from God. He decided that he didn't need God, that he was greater than his Creator, a wrong decision based on wrong information.

The enemy is defeated and destined to eternal damnation. Like any "good" sore loser, he wants others to go down with him. Upon eviction from Heaven, he took one third of the angels with him. They too are eternally doomed. His target now is mankind. He wants to prove that mankind was not even worth the sacrifice of Jesus on Calvary. He wants to minimize the power of the shed Blood of Jesus Christ. Yet another wrong decision based on wrong information. It is, was, and always will be impossible to minimize the power of the Blood of Jesus Christ!

Mankind is worth the sacrifice simply because God loves us! There is nothing that we have to do to make God love us. He loves us with an unending, far-reaching, ever-giving and forgiving love. John 3:16 says that God loves us and that's why He sent His Son to die for us on Calvary. Jesus arose from the dead and is now seated on the right hand of God the Father in Heaven.

He declared that it is finished! Jesus had the last say, the work can not be minimized or nullified. To the chagrin of the enemy, the battle has already been won! The enemy now is committed to deceiving mankind into making wrong decisions based on wrong information.

> Mankind is worth the sacrifice simply because God loves us!

It began in the Garden of Eden with Eve and Adam. Wrong decision based on wrong information. It is always the same modus operandi (method of operation). Get mankind to make a wrong decision based on wrong information. The ultimate wrong decision would be to end one's life. If this were to occur, the enemy would not have to worry about any future comebacks in faith. Your effectiveness would be nullified, your potential exterminated. Additionally, the ripple effect could cause depression, hopelessness, fear, bitterness, and a plethora of other bondages in other people.

Suicide is an act of desperation, a wrong decision based on wrong information. Your suicide will not make life easier for anyone else because they will no longer have the burden of caring for you. It will not be the easy way out of your current pain. Your situation is not hopeless. God has not forgotten about you. God is indeed able to intervene in the mess you are in and create victory for you. You matter to God. Jesus does want you. God is not mad at you. Whatever you have done, God will forgive you and re-write the script of your life.

You have not gone too far. You are not beyond the point of turning back. You are not bad. You may have made wrong decisions based on wrong information but as long as there is life there is hope. Ecclesiastes 9:4 says that anyone who is among the living has hope, even a live dog is better off than a dead lion! God will turn the situation around. Do not allow the enemy to persuade you into making a wrong decision based on wrong information.

Reject worry and fear. Accept Jesus and trust in His promise. He promised never to leave you. He promised to work all things together for your good. He promised that He knows the plans that He has for you, plans to give you a future and a hope. Be RELEASED from thoughts of suicide! In Jesus' name.

<u>NEXT STEPS</u>

God loves you. God is so powerful; He can undo whatever you have done or undo the negative effect of whatever has been done to you. God has this really marvelous way of taking what seemed like the worst thing ever and transforming it into the best thing ever. God is the original recycler. He will take something (or someone) that could be viewed as worthless, useless, outdated and or antiquated and find a new use for it. It will become priceless to someone, useful, valid and cutting edge. He has done this with people before. He has taken liars, murderers, cheaters, the sexually promiscuous, drunkards, cowards, racists, sexists, mentally challenged, physically challenged, the broken hearted, the heart breakers, hoarders, those who hold secrets, those who told secrets and a host of other less than perfect people and transformed them into marvelous examples of His restoring love. Give Him a chance; I declare that you are RELEASED from thoughts of suicide!

PRACTICAL APPLICATION

Recognize thoughts of suicide for what they really are. They are whisperings from the enemy to end your effectiveness. You may say that your effectiveness already ended, if that were true then the enemy would not be wasting time trying to move you off the scene. Truth is, you have more potential than you realize. More potential to create positive change in your life and in the lives of those around you. There is more for you to do. I know it is hard for you to believe that now. Why is it so much easier to believe the opposite? Pray for God to show you the truth. Read the Bible, it is truth. Accept the love around you. God has strategically positioned some people around you for this very moment. Receive their love. If you pray God will reveal them to you. You may already know who they are. Talk to one of them right now. Let them know what is going on with you. Don't try to handle this alone-God can work through people. Declare that you will live and not die! Refuse to entertain thoughts that are contrary to that declaration. In the name of Jesus Christ I declare that you are RELEASED!

I shall not die, but live, And declare the works of the Lord. (Psalms 118:17 KJV)

WWW (What Went Well)

Use this page to notate what went well as you made practical application of the next steps being RELEASED from THOUGHTS OF SUICIDE.

Dear...

What would you say if you had to write a note of encouragement to someone who needs to be RELEASED from Thoughts of Suicide?

154

<u>Lest We Forget</u>

Use this section to write a poem or other piece for recitation, compose a song, draw a cartoon, take a photograph and tape it here or any other type of creative expression that will trigger remembrance of the need to remain RELEASED from THOUGHTS OF SUICIDE.

Purposeful Prayer

Incorporate what you have learned into your daily prayers. Locate relevant scriptures and write them down as you commit them to memory for inclusion in times of prayer.

FINAL WORDS

Now you recognize the areas of confinement in your life and you know how to target your attention and prayers. You may have been nudged to assist someone else in identifying confining situations in their life. Give this book as a gift. Let them know that you were personally challenged. You don't have to go into specifics if you don't feel comfortable. Just let them know that this is a work of wisdom. Since you have confronted the areas of confinement in your life don't ever allow yourself to be lulled back into a state of non-awareness. Reread this work as you continue through life's journey. Take each chapter and journal your personal reflections about that captor. Research scriptures and pray for God to give you wisdom about who you can pray for and with. You have been released so that you can now reach others with this roadmap to freedom. Be the Harriet Tubman. Now that you have found the way out go back and leads others out. Pray and ask God to reveal others who need you to intercede in prayer for them about these captors (chapters). Integrate each of these chapters into your prayer life. Pray that none of your family or friends will ever be imprisoned by these captors. Pray that if any of your family or friends is already being held by these captors, that they be RELEASED right now by the Power of the Blood of Jesus Christ. Pray for future generations, that these captors will never have dominion over anyone in your bloodline. Use this work of wisdom as a roadmap for this and future generations to be RELEASED.

Rev. JaSina Barber Wise is an ordained minister of the Gospel of Jesus Christ. She is the founder of Beauty4Ashes, a fellowship of women, crossing the boundaries of race, age, economic status, sexual orientation, and political affiliation.

She and her daughter Eva are co-founders of B4Kids - a social outreach for youth. Rev. Wise and her son are co-founders of NJ's Turn, an initiative addressing the needs of the oldest sibling in divorced families. She has recorded with several groups and is a much sought after preacher, conference speaker, social activist and prophetic psalmist.

Rev. Wise, an avid reader and prolific writer, has penned several op-eds and poems. She has worked with several local, national, and international organizations that promote and unity between different faiths and backgrounds, equitable living conditions, and enhanced quality of life for all people. JaSina has travelled and spoken extensively in North America and Kenya.

Made in the USA
Middletown, DE
17 April 2015